THE MAXIMIZED LIFE COACHING & MENTORING
WINNING TEAM MODEL
(8-WEEK SERIES)
1st Edition

Ti'Juana A. Gholson

MAX Publishing, LLC

The Maximized Life Coaching & Mentoring Winning Team Model – 8-Week Series

1st Edition

Copyright 2020 by Ti'Juana Gholson

All rights reserved worldwide.

No part of this publication may be reproduced or transmitted in any form or by any means electronic or mechanical, including photocopying, recording, or any information storage and retrieval system without written permission from the author.

Published by MAX Publishing, LLC

Published in the United States of America.

ISBN: 13:978-1-970097-10-8

Disclaimer/Warning:

This book is intended for lecture and educational purposes only.

This program provides no guarantee of effectiveness for ALL persons.

This book/manual is the opinion of the writer and serves as a guide to support the lecture or training offered by the writer and team.

Book Cover Illustrations:	Trevor Lucas, Anomaly Studios
Editor:	Lawrence A. Gholson II, YOU Factor Coaching

The MAXIMIZED Life Coaching & Mentoring Winning Team Model walks the new and hopeful business owner through the basic steps of starting a business. Week one of this 8-week course starts with an orientation, which jumps right into mentorship and then walks the hopeful business owner through seven additional weeks of business preparation. The model is designed to provide one to one support to increase the likelihood of business start-up. Upon completion of the program, the new business owner is equipped with connections, practical business start-up information, and the tools to open the doors of their business.

ORIENTATION – An introduction to the Winning Team Model 8-Week Series

- Week 1 -   Mentorship
- Week 2 -   Legal
- Week 3 -   Banking
- Week 4 -   Accounting
- Week 5 -   Insurance
- Week 6 -   Human Resources
- Week 7 -   Real Estate
- Week 8 -   Marketing/Public Relations, IT & Virtual Assistance

THE MAXIMIZED LIFE COACHING & MENTORING WINNING TEAM MODEL
8-Week Series

THE MAXIMIZED LIFE COACHING & MENTORING WINNING TEAM MODEL
8-Week Series

WELCOME, Business Owner!

You have just taken the first step to pursuing your dream of becoming a business owner. Business entrepreneurship offers both fruitful and rewarding paths; however, there are tricks to the trade that if you are aware and can conquer on the front end will help you avoid unnecessary mistakes on the back end.

Starting a business can be both confusing and lonely so the hopes are that this course helps you replace confusion with the tools to be successful. Problem solving is what an entrepreneur does. That's why we, as business coaches, aim to assist you with solving as many business start-up challenges as we can. Be sure to attend each week, follow each step, ask as many questions of your coaches as you need to and use this guide to keep great notes and record your journey.

TRUST us… if you stay on top of your important tasks now, you are sure to operate a successful business later.

Enjoy the journey, have FUN and…

Let's DO Business!

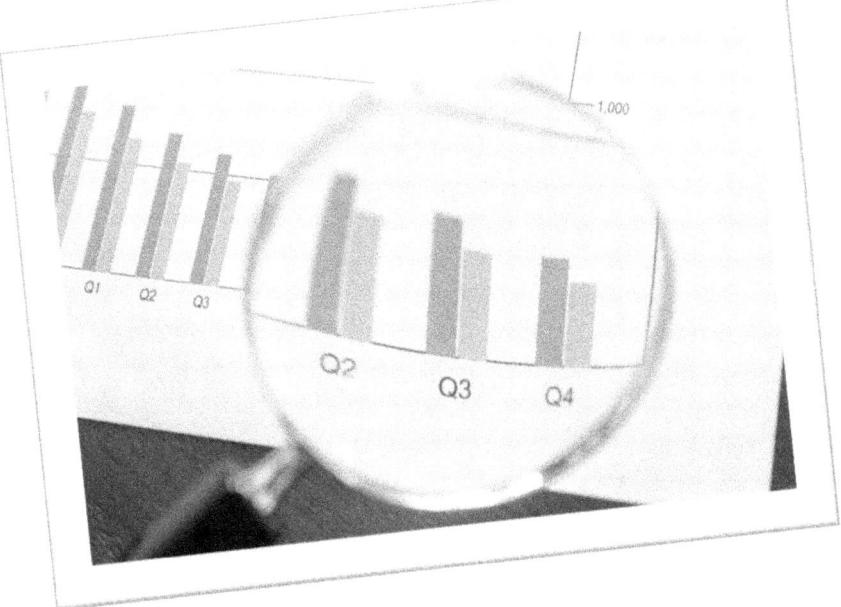

THE MAXIMIZED LIFE COACHING & MENTORING WINNING TEAM MODEL
8-Week Series

THE MAXIMIZED LIFE COACHING & MENTORING WINNING TEAM MODEL
8-Week Series

ORIENTATION

OBJECTIVES:

1. Program Overview
2. Introduction into Mentorship
    a. What is Business Coaching & Mentoring?
    b. How can the Business Owner use Business Coaching & Mentoring?
3. Introduction to Key Players in Business

Local Government	State Government	Federal Government
• City Hall • City Officials • Chamber of Commerce • Health Department • Zoning	• Employment Comission • State Corporation Commission • State Tax Administration • Any required state licensing office	• IRS.gov • Small Business Administration - sba.gov • Economic Development Administration eda.gov • Workforce Development (a combination of local, state and federal offices) • Any required federal licensing office

4. Your Business' Winning Team

    a. Each participant receives a manual which serves as a guide through the program and a business journal to record important information and to track their journey to business ownership. The manual helps the participant keep an organized list of their Winning Team partners as well as record their experiences as they are completing the 8-week series.

THE MAXIMIZED LIFE COACHING & MENTORING WINNING TEAM MODEL
8-Week Series

JOURNAL ENTRY:

WRITE YOUR FEELINGS AFTER ATTENDING THE ORIENTATION SESSION

How do you feel after attending orientation (discuss your excitement, fears, regrets, etc.)?

_____
_____
_____
_____
_____
_____
_____
_____
_____
_____
_____
_____
_____
_____
_____
_____
_____
_____
_____
_____

Will you commit to the 8-week sessions?   YES   NO
(Circle One)

Signature: _____ Date: _____/_____/_____

THE MAXIMIZED LIFE COACHING & MENTORING WINNING TEAM MODEL
8-Week Series

MENTORSHIP

Having someone to bounce ideas off in the beginning stages of business ownership is essential! Many hopeful entrepreneurs are the first in their family and are pioneering new ideas that their primary circle of influence (friends and family) is not familiar with.

Mentorship is key for any business owner. Having someone who has experienced what the new business owner is experiencing and has the wisdom to share is priceless to any new business owner.

Max Coaches/Mentors are in place to walk alongside the new business owner to help not only cheer them on but be that support when a roadblock or difficult situation arises. The Max Coach/Mentor will guide the new business owner and connect them with the appropriate professionals needed to develop what we call the "Winning Team". The Coach/Mentor is a part of that Winning Team, just as an Attorney, Accountant, Banker, Insurance Professional, Human Resource Professional, Realtor, Marketing Professional, IT Professional and Assistant/Virtual Assistant.

This week's session will discuss what a coach/mentor is, the mentee/mentor relationship, what to expect over the next few weeks from your coach/mentor and much more.

Let's DO Business!

THE MAXIMIZED LIFE COACHING & MENTORING WINNING TEAM MODEL
8-Week Series

THE MAXIMIZED LIFE COACHING & MENTORING WINNING TEAM MODEL
8-Week Series

WEEK 1 – MENTORSHIP

OBJECTIVES:

- Definition of Coaching/Mentorship

- Business Plan - Creating the Vision/Mission Statement; Goal Setting & Developing a Business Plan

- Budget and Projections - The Startup Budget (brainstorming)

This session will discuss:

- My Coach/Mentor Name:

- My Coach/Mentor Contact information:

    Phone:
    Email:_____

- 1st Coach/Mentor Meeting Date: _____/_____/_____ Time: _____ am/pm
- Business Plan developing start date: _____/_____/_____
- Business Plan completion date: _____/_____/_____
- Budget development start date: _____/_____/_____
- Budget development completion date: _____/_____/_____

NOTES:

THE MAXIMIZED LIFE COACHING & MENTORING WINNING TEAM MODEL
8-Week Series

JOURNAL ENTRY:

WRITE YOUR FEELINGS AFTER ATTENDING THE MENTORSHIP SESSION

How do you feel after attending the mentorship session (discuss your excitement, fears, regrets, etc.)?

_____
_____
_____
_____
_____
_____
_____
_____
_____
_____
_____
_____
_____
_____
_____
_____
_____
_____
_____
_____

Will you commit to working with a coach/mentor during your business startup journey?

                    YES   NO

                 (Circle One)

Signature: _____ Date: _____/_____/_____

THE MAXIMIZED LIFE COACHING & MENTORING WINNING TEAM MODEL
8-Week Series

Let's Brainstorm:

WHAT type of business are you opening?

WHY do you wish to open this type of business?

WHO is your customer?

WHEN do you plan to open your business doors?

WHERE do you plan to do business?

HOW will you accomplish this?

List 3 of your MAJOR Business Goals:
1.
2.
3.

Will you commit to developing your business plan and budget?   YES   NO
(Circle One)

Signature: _____   Date: _____/_____/_____

THE MAXIMIZED LIFE COACHING & MENTORING WINNING TEAM MODEL
8-Week Series

LIST ANY ADDITIONAL BUSINESS GOALS HERE:

THE MAXIMIZED LIFE COACHING & MENTORING WINNING TEAM MODEL
8-Week Series

THE SAMPLE BUSINESS PLAN

COVERSHEET

_____

(BUSINESS NAME)

Business Plan

_____, Owner

Created on ____/____/_____

THE MAXIMIZED LIFE COACHING & MENTORING WINNING TEAM MODEL
8-Week Series

Executive Summary

Product

YOUR COMPANY NAME _____ provides _____. Our services include _____.

Customers

The target audience for our company is _____

Future of the Company

_____ is a fast-paced, evolving industry. In response to this, _____ will offer other services, including _____ in the future.

Company Description

Mission Statement

To _____.

Principal Members

_____ — Owner
_____ — Co-Owner
_____ — CFO

Legal Structure

_____ is an _____ (i.e., LLC, LLP, Inc, S Corporation, C Corporation, etc.) Corporation - incorporated in _____,
_____. _____.
          City   State

THE MAXIMIZED LIFE COACHING & MENTORING WINNING TEAM MODEL
8-Week Series

Market Research

Industry

_____ will join the _____ industry. (DISCUSS YOUR INDUSTRY).

Businesses like ours also have a history of working with _____

A recent study stated that _____ industry is projected to grow by _____% per year for the next several years.

Detailed Description of Customers

The target customers for _____ are _____. Specifically, we specialize in _____. To capitalize on opportunities that are geographically close as we start and grow our business, _____ will specifically target _____. This will allow us to take advantage of the company's proximity to _____.

Company Advantages

Our advantages are:

- We maintain quality customer service.
- We _____
- We _____

Regulations

_____ must meet all Federal and state regulations concerning _____. Specifically, _____.

THE MAXIMIZED LIFE COACHING & MENTORING WINNING TEAM MODEL
8-Week Series

Service Line

Product/Service

Product/Services Include:

- _____ Products or Services

- _____

- _____

Pricing Structure

_____ will offer products at a cost of _____ OR services at an hourly rate of _____.

Product Lifecycle

All products OR services are ready to be offered to clients.

Intellectual Property Rights

_____ is a trademarked name in the state of _____, and we have filed for protection of our proprietary processes and other intellectual property, such as our logo. We have also registered our domain name and parked relevant social media accounts for future use and to prevent the likelihood of someone impersonating our brand.

Research and Development

The company is planning to conduct the following research and development:

- Determine the need for additional services within our market related to _____.

- Find trends in _____ that may provide potentially competitive in order to ensure _____ continues to carefully carve its niche in the marketplace.

THE MAXIMIZED LIFE COACHING & MENTORING WINNING TEAM MODEL
8-Week Series

Marketing & Sales

Growth Strategy

To grow the company, _____ will do the following:

(SEE SAMPLES BELOW)

- **Network** at _____ conferences
- **Establish a company website** that contains engaging multimedia content about our goods OR services
- As the business grows, **advertise in various platforms and publications** that reach our target industries

Communicate with the Customer

_____ will communicate with its customers by:

(SEE SAMPLES BELOW)

- Interacting in person in the store/office.
- Using social media such as Instagram, Snap Chat, Twitter, YouTube, Facebook, Tik Tok, and LinkedIn
- Providing contact information on the company website

How to Sell

Currently, the person in charge of sales for _____ is the (TITLE)_____, _____ (NAME). As profits increase, _____ will look to add an employee to assist with _____.
This individual will also provide company social media and online marketing support. The company will increase awareness to our targeted customers through online advertising, proactive public relations campaigns, and attending tradeshows.

THE MAXIMIZED LIFE COACHING & MENTORING WINNING TEAM MODEL
8-Week Series

THE SAMPLE STARTUP BUDGET

INCOME	EXPENSE CATEGORY	EXPENSE COST
Revenue Source	**State Filing Fees** (Corporation Commission Fees) i.e., LLC, INC, Fictitious Name fees	
	Banking Fees	
	Legal Fees: Operating Agreement	
	Legal Fees: Articles of Incorporation	
	City Fees: Business License	
	Accounting Fees - i.e., QuickBooks start up	
	Insurance	
	Lease – i.e., deposit, first month rent, utilities	
	Marketing	
	IT	
	Assistant/Virtual Assistant	
	Equipment - i.e., computers, printers, copy machines	
	Furniture - i.e., desks, chairs	
	Supplies – i.e., paper, ink, pens, paperclips	
	Carry Over – a cushion for the company	
	Misc.	
TOTAL		

THE MAXIMIZED LIFE COACHING & MENTORING WINNING TEAM MODEL
8-Week Series

LEGAL:

Many businesses fail to seek legal counsel during the beginning stages. New entrepreneurs negate this step out of fear of not being able to pay an attorney. They THINK that they can do it alone making the mistake of entering contracts and setting up their business structure themselves to find it incorrectly done.

Another area the new entrepreneur miss is having a discussion of what happens to the business if they are no longer able to run it. The new entrepreneur rarely plans the future health of their business. What happens if the business owner gets ill, or simply wishes to retire from the business? What happens to all the hard work the business owner put into the business? What happens to the business itself? This discussion is called an exit strategy, estate, or succession planning. Many new entrepreneurs do not know or do not even think of this topic however it is a great place to start if planning to be in business long-term.

This session will help the participant think long-term. It will help plan with the end goal in mind working backwards covering all foundational areas first before launching your business.

This session aims to assure that the participant is introduced to an attorney BEFORE finalizing a decision of what business structure to choose.

THE MAXIMIZED LIFE COACHING & MENTORING WINNING TEAM MODEL

8-Week Series

THE MAXIMIZED LIFE COACHING & MENTORING WINNING TEAM MODEL
8-Week Series

WEEK 2 – LEGAL

OBJECTIVES:

- Business Structure: How to select the best structure for your business
- Contracts: when does the business owner need to get an attorney involved
- Succession/Estate Planning: Protecting your business from the beginning

This session will discuss:

- The various business structures (i.e., Inc., LLC, LLP, etc.)
- Business contracts
- Succession/Estate Planning: Protecting your business legacy

NOTES:

THE MAXIMIZED LIFE COACHING & MENTORING WINNING TEAM MODEL
8-Week Series

WRITE YOUR FEELINGS AFTER ATTENDING THE LEGAL SESSION

How do you feel after attending the legal session (discuss your excitement, fears, regrets, etc.)?

_____
_____
_____
_____
_____
_____
_____
_____
_____
_____
_____
_____
_____
_____
_____
_____
_____
_____
_____
_____

Will you commit to meeting with an attorney before moving forward with business plans?

YES   NO

(Circle One)

Signature: _____ Date: ____/____/____

THE MAXIMIZED LIFE COACHING & MENTORING WINNING TEAM MODEL
8-Week Series

BANKING/FUNDING:

A relationship with a banker can change the course of how a business does business. No business can go far without first funding it. A business owner can have the greatest plan in the world and the motivation to go with it; however, if there are no funds there will be no FUN in business! A good banking relationship is the difference between access to capital (OPM) to grow or the business only being able to take their business to a certain point.

A business owner must also face the state of their personal financial health. Yes, that is normally the elephant in the room. However, in the beginning stages of business the business owner usually co-signs for the business until the business has grown its own credit.

This session will help the participant explore why a good banking relationship is important as well as delve into the personal and discuss not only business credit but the business owner's personal credit. If the business owner plans to hire staff one day, he/she must assure the basics of managing money is conquered. This financial conquering starts with the business owner himself/herself.

There may be other funding sources available also. A good relationship with your local Small Business Administration (SBA) office, the local Economic Development (EDA) office, and local Workforce Development offices may serve as good resources for you. However, it is imperative that your business financial records are maintained and up to date as well as *you,* the business owner, maintain good credit.

THE MAXIMIZED LIFE COACHING & MENTORING WINNING TEAM MODEL
8-Week Series

THE MAXIMIZED LIFE COACHING & MENTORING WINNING TEAM MODEL
8-Week Series

WEEK 3 – BANKING/FUNDING

OBJECTIVES:

- Credit: a discussion of personal and business credit- annualcreditreport.com & dnb.com
- Business Banking: the relationship between a bank and a business
- Introduction to the Small Business Administration (SBA) – sba.gov
- Introduction to the Economic Development Administration (EDA) – eda.gov

This session will discuss:

- Credit Reporting: The business owner knowing their credit status; downloading the credit report and working on any credit issues
- Business credit: registering with a business credit reporting agency (i.e., Dunn & Bradstreet)
- Banking Relationship: Building a relationship with a banker
- The resources of the SBA
- The resources of the EDA

NOTES:

THE MAXIMIZED LIFE COACHING & MENTORING WINNING TEAM MODEL
8-Week Series

WRITE YOUR FEELINGS AFTER ATTENDING THE BANKING/FUNDING SESSION

How do you feel after attending the banking/funding session (discuss your excitement, fears, regrets, etc.)?

_____
_____
_____
_____
_____
_____
_____
_____
_____
_____
_____
_____
_____
_____
_____
_____
_____
_____
_____
_____

Will you commit to meeting with a banker to establish a relationship?   YES   NO

(Circle One)

Signature: _____   Date: ____/____/____

THE MAXIMIZED LIFE COACHING & MENTORING WINNING TEAM MODEL
8-Week Series

ACCOUNTING:

An Accountant is the most forgotten member of the winning team. Most business owners think they cannot afford an accountant when in fact they cannot afford NOT to have one. Many successful business owners will tell you it is fine to manage the business funds in the beginning; however, as the business grows, you as the new business owner, cannot keep up with all the laws around taxes that a Certified Public Accountant MUST stay abreast of.

Trying to deal with tax laws and the IRS on your own is never a wise business move. You will find that having to pay on the back end for an accountant to clean up poor record keeping is not worth it. Also, note the difference between a Certified Public Accountant (CPA) and a Bookkeeper. A Bookkeeper can help you maintain your financial records on a day-to-day basis by making journal entries of sales and purchases. However, if that Bookkeeper is not a CPA, they may not know tax laws and other laws to help your business maintain and grow. That Bookkeeper also may not be able to properly assist when it is time to file taxes and assure proper deductions and filing. Therefore, best practice is to start out forming

a relationship with a CPA. Please believe that it will save you in the long run!

This session will introduce the participant to the idea of having a CPA on their Winning Team and establishing a business start-up budget.

THE MAXIMIZED LIFE COACHING & MENTORING WINNING TEAM MODEL

8-Week Series

THE MAXIMIZED LIFE COACHING & MENTORING WINNING TEAM MODEL
8-Week Series

WEEK 4 – ACCOUNTING

OBJECTIVES:

- Importance of having a Certified Public Accountant (CPA)
- Business Taxes (state, federal, employment, social security, sales, etc.)
- Payroll service and their role in business
- The business start-up budget

This session will discuss:

- CPA: The role of a CPA on the business team
- Taxes: Business taxes and an introduction of the various type of taxes a business pays
- Payroll: Payroll and the role a payroll company plays in business
- Budget: Basic budget line items in the business budget

NOTES:

THE MAXIMIZED LIFE COACHING & MENTORING WINNING TEAM MODEL
8-Week Series

WRITE YOUR FEELINGS AFTER ATTENDING THE ACCOUNTING SESSION

How do you feel after attending the accounting session (discuss your excitement, fears, regrets, etc.)?

_____
_____
_____
_____
_____
_____
_____
_____
_____
_____
_____
_____
_____
_____
_____
_____
_____
_____
_____
_____
_____

Will you commit to meeting with an accountant to establish a relationship?   YES   NO

(Circle One)

Signature: _____   Date: _____/_____/_____

THE MAXIMIZED LIFE COACHING & MENTORING WINNING TEAM MODEL
8-Week Series

INSURANCE:

Securing your business is one of the best actions a business owner can take. Business insurance protects your business from financial failure in case of incident or misbehavior by employees. Business insurance to protect your space, equipment and supplies are also recommended, as unforeseen damages could happen in the business space just like in a home.

Another recommended option that many business owners fail to take advantage of is insuring themselves or another key player in the company in case of loss. Yes, it may be a good idea to insure yourself especially if you are what is called the "key man" in your business and the business needs someone like YOU to keep it running. That is why we recommend that you, as a business owner, not only have a relationship with a business insurance professional but have a relationship with a financial planner as well.

The financial planner will help you plan for the future of your business, as well as help you preserve your family's business legacy (just like the attorney). Working with a financial planner helps you to look ahead to the future and the goal of planning for an exit strategy as every busines owner should consider planning for the future of their business and one day passing it on.

This session will help the participant explore future plans for business, looking at both securing the business and securing the business owner.

THE MAXIMIZED LIFE COACHING & MENTORING WINNING TEAM MODEL

8-Week Series

THE MAXIMIZED LIFE COACHING & MENTORING WINNING TEAM MODEL
8-Week Series

WEEK 5 – INSURANCE/FINANCIAL PLANNING

OBJECTIVES:

- Business Insurance: The importance of insuring a business
- Business Insurance: The types of insurance a business need
- Financial Planning: Planning for the financial future of the business by protecting the business owner and the business legacy

This session will discuss business insurance types such as:

- Professional
- Liability
- Property (Building / Structure)
- Equipment
- Vehicular

Business Protection Insurance such as:

- Keyman
- Long-Term Care

NOTES:

THE MAXIMIZED LIFE COACHING & MENTORING WINNING TEAM MODEL
8-Week Series

WRITE YOUR FEELINGS AFTER ATTENDING THE INSURANCE/FINANCIAL PLANNING SESSION

How do you feel after attending the insurance/financial planning session (discuss your excitement, fears, regrets, etc.)?

_____
_____
_____
_____
_____
_____
_____
_____
_____
_____
_____
_____
_____
_____
_____
_____
_____
_____
_____
_____

Will you commit to meeting with an insurance professional and financial planner to establish a relationship?   YES   NO

(Circle One)

Signature: _____   Date: _____/_____/_____

THE MAXIMIZED LIFE COACHING & MENTORING WINNING TEAM MODEL
8-Week Series

HUMAN RESOURCES:

Human Resources, an often-missed area, is another essential department in business. Most small businesses think they can simply hire staff, pay them, and fire them when things do not go right. WRONG!

There are many laws and rules pertaining to hiring and firing. A great start for any business owner is to connect with the local employment commission. However, having a full-time human resource professional is IDEAL. Reality may say that many small businesses are not able to hire a full-time Human Resource specialist in the beginning and that is alright. Yet, a new business owner should at least hire the consultation of a Human Resource Professional.

There are many consulting firms available now that can assist the small business owner with setting up personnel files, assuring employee handbooks and personnel manuals are within the law and be a support in times of conflict, hiring and firing. There are many laws around equal employment and what a business can or cannot do. Thus, it is imperative that any new business owner has on their team the right Human Resource Consultant who is familiar with these laws.

This session will help the participant explore why human resources is an essential part of their business.

THE MAXIMIZED LIFE COACHING & MENTORING WINNING TEAM MODEL
8-Week Series

THE MAXIMIZED LIFE COACHING & MENTORING WINNING TEAM MODEL
8-Week Series

WEEK 6 – HUMAN RESOURCES

OBJECTIVES:

- What are Human Resources and what role does Human Resources plays in business
- The importance of establishing a Human Resources Professional relationship
- Introduction to the employment commission and the role it plays in business

This session will discuss

- Human Resource essentials for a new business
- The benefits of being connected to a Human Resource Professional
- Company's legal responsibility (employment commission requirements)

NOTES:

THE MAXIMIZED LIFE COACHING & MENTORING WINNING TEAM MODEL
8-Week Series

WRITE YOUR FEELINGS AFTER ATTENDING THE HUMAN RESOURCES SESSION

How do you feel after attending the Human Resource session (discuss your excitement, fears, regrets, etc.)?

_____
_____
_____
_____
_____
_____
_____
_____
_____
_____
_____
_____
_____
_____
_____
_____
_____
_____
_____

Will you commit to meeting with a Human Resource Professional to establish a relationship?
YES   NO

(Circle One)

Signature: _____   Date: ____/____/____

THE MAXIMIZED LIFE COACHING & MENTORING WINNING TEAM MODEL
8-Week Series

REAL ESTATE:

Don't' be fooled!

Commercial real estate leasing is NOT as simple as renting an apartment or home for personal use. Commercial leasing agreements have many terms that could cause a new business owner to suffer financial hardship if they are not careful. Not only does the small business owner need to consult an attorney for contracting but also a commercial realtor, someone familiar with commercial leasing and commercial leasing terminology.

Many commercial leases include items that are not included in residential leases. There are items such sales percentage fees and Common Area Maintenance Fees (CAM) that many new business owners are not aware of. Not counting the costs before leasing and being surprised with the fees each month could cause an upset in the budget. Many new business owners are not familiar with these types of fees and find themselves surprised when they are hit with additional charges throughout the month. Those additional charges could be the difference between paying staff or keeping the doors open. That is an extremely uncomfortable situation for new business owners to be in so… consult the professionals!

This session will introduce the participant to a Realtor.

THE MAXIMIZED LIFE COACHING & MENTORING WINNING TEAM MODEL
8-Week Series

THE MAXIMIZED LIFE COACHING & MENTORING WINNING TEAM MODEL
8-Week Series

WEEK 7 – REAL ESTATE

OBJECTIVES:

- Connecting and having a relationship with a Realtor (Commercial & Residential)
- Selecting the right location to do business
- Interpreting/Navigating a commercial lease

This session will discuss:

- Difference between Commercial and Residential Realtors
- How to select "The Right" location
- Leasing: What is common in commercial leasing (contracts)

NOTES:

THE MAXIMIZED LIFE COACHING & MENTORING WINNING TEAM MODEL
8-Week Series

WRITE YOUR FEELINGS AFTER ATTENDING THE REAL ESTATE SESSION

How do you feel after attending the real estate session (discuss your excitement, fears, regrets, etc.)?

_____
_____
_____
_____
_____
_____
_____
_____
_____
_____
_____
_____
_____
_____
_____
_____
_____
_____
_____
_____
_____
_____
_____

Will you commit to meeting with a Realtor to establish a relationship?   YES   NO

(Circle One)

Signature: _____   Date: _____ / _____ / _____

THE MAXIMIZED LIFE COACHING & MENTORING WINNING TEAM MODEL
8-Week Series

MARKETING/PUBLIC RELATIONS, IT & VIRTUAL ASSISTANCE:

MARKETING/PR: Okay, now that you have established your business and the doors are open, WHO knows you exist? Marketing/Public Relations is another overlooked area in business. Some business owners falsely believe people will enter their establishment without invitation. Some will, but the masses will not. Much goes into preparing the public for the business's arrival. If you watch how a major chain or a franchise does it, marketing takes place the entire time even during construction. It can be as simple as a coming soon sign, a soft TV commercial or a local mailer. Marketing MUST take place to get foot traffic.

Many business owners feel as though they cannot afford a marketing consultant… we say if you wish to stay in busines, you cannot afford NOT to have one. Do not be fooled, it takes a LOT to get the customer in the doors and then it takes great customer service to get them to buy and return.

IT: If a business wishes to take their business to another level, simplify systems, stay cutting edge, it may be a good idea to have an IT professional on the team. IT professionals can help with all the networking issues that will arise, from connecting your computer systems, to assuring

THE MAXIMIZED LIFE COACHING & MENTORING WINNING TEAM MODEL
8-Week Series

all your systems sync. They can also work with your web developer and other team members to assure continuity in your systems.

VA: What is a Virtual Assistant you say? Why would I need one, I am just a one man show? Many business owners think because they are small and are the sole employee, they can do everything themselves. The excitement of business ownership and wanting to oversee everything often clouds their judgment. The new business owner's excitement does not make them think of burn-out, which is REAL. Burn-out can cause a new business owner to no longer *enjoy* their business. That is where a Virtual Assistant can help.

A Virtual Assistant (VA) is an extra pair of hands. Again, another part of the team that business owners overlook for fear of not being able to afford. A VA can be the savior of any business. Imagine getting more done if you had someone behind the scenes handling the busy work for you. One phone call and an owner can lose a whole day. However, if they had an assistant to take the phone calls, do the typing, arrange the appointments, monitor social media, and complete any other tasks that keeps the business owner from doing business, much more meaningful business tasks could get done.

This session will educate the participant on how marketing can help a business grow, how IT is an essential department, and how having a Virtual Assistant can save the new business owner from burn-out.

THE MAXIMIZED LIFE COACHING & MENTORING WINNING TEAM MODEL
8-Week Series

WEEK 8 – MARKETING / PUBLIC RELATIONS / INFORMATION TECHNOLOGY / VIRTUAL ASSISTANT

OBJECTIVES:

- Marketing/PR: The importance of marketing & basic marketing strategies
- Information Technology: taking your business to another level with better technology
- Virtual Assistant: How can they help?

This session will discuss:

- Marketing: What is marketing and why the business owner needs it
- IT: How an Information Technology Professional can help to take your business further
- Virtual Assistant: How an assistant can help your company

NOTES:

THE MAXIMIZED LIFE COACHING & MENTORING WINNING TEAM MODEL
8-Week Series

WRITE YOUR FEELINGS AFTER ATTENDING THE MARKETING, IT & VIRTUAL ASSISTANT SESSION

How do you feel after attending the Marketing, IT & Virtual Assistant session (discuss your excitement, fears, regrets, etc.)?

_____
_____
_____
_____
_____
_____
_____
_____
_____
_____
_____
_____
_____
_____
_____
_____
_____
_____
_____
_____

Will you commit to meeting with a Marketing Professional, IT Professional & Virtual Assistant to establish a relationship?   YES   NO

(Circle One)

Signature: _____   Date: _____/_____/_____

THE MAXIMIZED LIFE COACHING & MENTORING WINNING TEAM MODEL
8-Week Series

CONGRATULATIONS!

You have completed the Maximized Life Coaching and Mentoring Winning Team Model 8-Week Session!

We are delighted to have spent these weeks with you. At this point, you may have either started your business or you are closer than you have ever been. We, the Maximized Life Team, are proud of you and are delighted that you took the time to attend this course. It is our desire that you were enriched, made many connections, and you are better prepared to move forward with your dream of business ownership. Keep this manual/journal as a tool to refer to when needed. Go back in a few weeks and look at the journal entries you wrote and compare today to where you were at that time. Measure your success and celebrate your accomplishments.

Again, we are proud of you and we wish you well on your journey of business ownership!

Let's DO Business!

The Maximized Life Coaching and Mentoring Team

THE MAXIMIZED LIFE COACHING & MENTORING WINNING TEAM MODEL
8-Week Series

MAX COACHES

MAXIMIZED Life Coaching & Mentoring 8-Week Winning Team program will:

- Provide trained coaches to the program that will assist the program participant (entrepreneur) with walking the path to business start-up using the MAX Coaching & Mentoring system.
- Serve as a model to the facilitated weekly sessions that provides start-up steps to opening a new business (this includes this manual/journal and supporting reading material).
- Suggest professional speakers for weekly sessions.

Supporting reading material & resources:

Girl WHAT you gonna DO with your MONEY!   Written by Ti'Juana A. Gholson

Mind on My Money   Written by Lawrence A. Gholson II

YOU Factor   Written by Lawrence A. Gholson II

THE MAXIMIZED LIFE COACHING & MENTORING WINNING TEAM MODEL
8-Week Series

FORMS

- Goal Sheets
- Budget Sheets
- Business Plan Format
- Inventory Form
- Business Contacts Organizing Sheets
- Journal Pages

THE MAXIMIZED LIFE COACHING & MENTORING WINNING TEAM MODEL
8-Week Series

Goal Sheets

List 3 of your MAJOR Business Goals:

1.
2.
3.

Long-term GOAL	OBJECTIVES	ACTION STEPS	START DATE	TARGET DATE

THE MAXIMIZED LIFE COACHING & MENTORING WINNING TEAM MODEL

THE MAXIMIZED LIFE COACHING & MENTORING WINNING TEAM MODEL
8-Week Series

Goal Sheets

List 3 of your MAJOR Business Goals:

1.

2.

3.

Long-term GOAL	OBJECTIVES	ACTION STEPS	START DATE	TARGET DATE

THE MAXIMIZED LIFE COACHING & MENTORING WINNING TEAM MODEL
8-Week Series

Goal Sheets

List 3 of your MAJOR Business Goals:

1.
2.
3.

Long-term GOAL	OBJECTIVES	ACTION STEPS	START DATE	TARGET DATE

THE MAXIMIZED LIFE COACHING & MENTORING WINNING TEAM MODEL
8-Week Series

THE SAMPLE STARTUP BUDGET

INCOME	EXPENSE CATEGORY	EXPENSE COST
Revenue Source	State Filing Fees (Corporation Commission Fees) i.e., LLC, INC, Fictitious Name fees	
	Banking Fees	
	Legal Fees: Operating Agreement	
	Legal Fees: Articles of Incorporation	
	City Fees: Business License	
	Accounting Fees - i.e., QuickBooks start up	
	Insurance	
	Lease – i.e., deposit, first month rent, utilities	
	Marketing	
	IT	
	Assistant/Virtual Assistant	
	Equipment - i.e., computers, printers, copy machines	
	Furniture - i.e., desks, chairs	
	Supplies – i.e., paper, ink, pens, paperclips	
	Carry Over – a cushion for the company	
	Misc.	
TOTAL		

THE MAXIMIZED LIFE COACHING & MENTORING WINNING TEAM MODEL
8-Week Series

THE SAMPLE STARTUP BUDGET

INCOME	EXPENSE CATEGORY	EXPENSE COST
Revenue Source	**State Filing Fees** (Corporation Commission Fees) i.e., LLC, INC, Fictitious Name fees	
	Banking Fees	
	Legal Fees: Operating Agreement	
	Legal Fees: Articles of Incorporation	
	City Fees: Business License	
	Accounting Fees - i.e., QuickBooks start up	
	Insurance	
	Lease – i.e., deposit, first month rent, utilities	
	Marketing	
	IT	
	Assistant/Virtual Assistant	
	Equipment - i.e., computers, printers, copy machines	
	Furniture - i.e., desks, chairs	
	Supplies – i.e., paper, ink, pens, paperclips	
	Carry Over – a cushion for the company	
	Misc.	
TOTAL		

THE MAXIMIZED LIFE COACHING & MENTORING WINNING TEAM MODEL
8-Week Series

THE SAMPLE STARTUP BUDGET

INCOME	EXPENSE CATEGORY	EXPENSE COST
Revenue Source	State Filing Fees (Corporation Commission Fees) i.e., LLC, INC, Fictitious Name fees	
	Banking Fees	
	Legal Fees: Operating Agreement	
	Legal Fees: Articles of Incorporation	
	City Fees: Business License	
	Accounting Fees - i.e., QuickBooks start up	
	Insurance	
	Lease – i.e., deposit, first month rent, utilities	
	Marketing	
	IT	
	Assistant/Virtual Assistant	
	Equipment - i.e., computers, printers, copy machines	
	Furniture - i.e., desks, chairs	
	Supplies – i.e., paper, ink, pens, paperclips	
	Carry Over – a cushion for the company	
	Misc.	
TOTAL		

THE MAXIMIZED LIFE COACHING & MENTORING WINNING TEAM MODEL
8-Week Series

THE SAMPLE STARTUP BUDGET

INCOME	EXPENSE CATEGORY	EXPENSE COST
Revenue Source	**State Filing Fees** (Corporation Commission Fees) i.e., LLC, INC, Fictitious Name fees	
	Banking Fees	
	Legal Fees: Operating Agreement	
	Legal Fees: Articles of Incorporation	
	City Fees: Business License	
	Accounting Fees - i.e., QuickBooks start up	
	Insurance	
	Lease – i.e., deposit, first month rent, utilities	
	Marketing	
	IT	
	Assistant/Virtual Assistant	
	Equipment - i.e., computers, printers, copy machines	
	Furniture - i.e., desks, chairs	
	Supplies – i.e., paper, ink, pens, paperclips	
	Carry Over – a cushion for the company	
	Misc.	
TOTAL		

THE MAXIMIZED LIFE COACHING & MENTORING WINNING TEAM MODEL
8-Week Series

THE SAMPLE BUSINESS PLAN

COVERSHEET

_____

(BUSINESS NAME)

Business Plan

_____, Owner

Created on _____/_____/_____

THE MAXIMIZED LIFE COACHING & MENTORING WINNING TEAM MODEL
8-Week Series

Executive Summary

Product

YOUR COMPANY NAME _____ provides _____. Our services include _____.

Customers

The target audience for our company is _____

Future of the Company

_____ is a fast-paced, evolving industry. In response to this, _____ will offer other services, including _____ in the future.

Company Description

Mission Statement

To _____.

Principal Members

_____ — Owner
_____ — Co-Owner
_____ — CFO

Legal Structure

_____ is an _____ (i.e., LLC, LLP, Inc, S Corporation, C Corporation, etc.) Corporation - incorporated in _____,
_____. _____.
             City   State

THE MAXIMIZED LIFE COACHING & MENTORING WINNING TEAM MODEL
8-Week Series

Market Research

Industry

_____ will join the _____ industry. (DISCUSS YOUR INDUSTRY).

Businesses like ours also have a history of working with _____

A recent study stated that _____ industry is projected to grow by _____% per year for the next several years.

Detailed Description of Customers

The target customers for _____ are _____. Specifically, we specialize in _____. To capitalize on opportunities that are geographically close as we start and grow our business, _____ will specifically target _____. This will allow us to take advantage of the company's proximity to _____.

Company Advantages

Our advantages are:

- We maintain quality customer service.
- We _____
- We _____

Regulations

_____ must meet all Federal and state regulations concerning _____. Specifically, _____.

THE MAXIMIZED LIFE COACHING & MENTORING WINNING TEAM MODEL
8-Week Series

Service Line

Product/Service

Product/Services Include:

- _____ Products or Services

- _____

- _____

Pricing Structure

_____ will offer products at a cost of _____ OR services at an hourly rate of _____.

Product Lifecycle

All products OR services are ready to be offered to clients.

Intellectual Property Rights

_____ is a trademarked name in the state of _____, and we have filed for protection of our proprietary processes and other intellectual property, such as our logo. We have also registered our domain name and parked relevant social media accounts for future use and to prevent the likelihood of someone impersonating our brand.

Research and Development

The company is planning to conduct the following research and development:

- Determine the need for additional services within our market related to _____.

- Find trends in _____ that may provide potentially competitive in order to ensure _____ continues to carefully carve its niche in the marketplace.

THE MAXIMIZED LIFE COACHING & MENTORING WINNING TEAM MODEL
8-Week Series

Marketing & Sales

Growth Strategy

To grow the company, _____ will do the following:

(SEE SAMPLES BELOW)

- **Network** at _____ conferences
- **Establish a company website** that contains engaging multimedia content about our goods OR services
- As the business grows, **advertise in various platforms and publications** that reach our target industries

Communicate with the Customer

_____ will communicate with its customers by:

(SEE SAMPLES BELOW)

- Interacting in person in the store/office.
- Using social media such as Instagram, Snap Chat, Twitter, YouTube, Facebook, and LinkedIn
- Providing contact information on the company website

How to Sell

Currently, the person in charge of sales for _____ is the (TITLE)_____, _____ (NAME). As profits increase, _____ will look to add an employee to assist with _____.
This individual will also provide company social media and online marketing support. The company will increase awareness to our targeted customers through online advertising, proactive public relations campaigns, and attending tradeshows.

THE MAXIMIZED LIFE COACHING & MENTORING WINNING TEAM MODEL
8-Week Series

Inventory Form

Item Description	QTY on Hand	Vendor/Supplier	Product Code/SKU	Order Date

THE MAXIMIZED LIFE COACHING & MENTORING WINNING TEAM MODEL
8-Week Series

Inventory Form

Item Description	QTY on Hand	Vendor/Supplier	Product Code/SKU	Order Date

THE MAXIMIZED LIFE COACHING & MENTORING WINNING TEAM MODEL
8-Week Series

Inventory Form

Item Description	QTY on Hand	Vendor/Supplier	Product Code/SKU	Order Date

THE MAXIMIZED LIFE COACHING & MENTORING WINNING TEAM MODEL
8-Week Series

Inventory Form

Item Description	QTY on Hand	Vendor/Supplier	Product Code/SKU	Order Date

THE MAXIMIZED LIFE COACHING & MENTORING WINNING TEAM MODEL
8-Week Series

Business Contacts

Professional	Name	Phone	Email	Web Site
Coach/Mentor				
Attorney				
Accountant				
Banker				
Insurance Professional				
Human Resource Professional				
Realtor				
Marketing Professional				
IT Professional				
Virtual Assistant/Assistant				
Workforce Development				
Economic Development				
Small Business Administration				

THE MAXIMIZED LIFE COACHING & MENTORING WINNING TEAM MODEL
8-Week Series

Business Contacts

Professional	Name	Phone	Email	Web Site
Coach/Mentor				
Attorney				
Accountant				
Banker				
Insurance Professional				
Human Resource Professional				
Realtor				
Marketing Professional				
IT Professional				
Virtual Assistant/Assistant				
Workforce Development				
Economic Development				
Small Business Administration				

THE MAXIMIZED LIFE COACHING & MENTORING WINNING TEAM MODEL
8-Week Series

JOURNAL ENTRY:

WRITE YOUR FEELINGS AS YOU CONTINUE YOUR JOURNEY TO BUSINESS OWNERSHIP

Date: ___/___/___ How do you feel about your business progress TODAY (discuss your excitement, fears, regrets, etc.)?

_____
_____
_____
_____
_____
_____
_____
_____
_____
_____
_____
_____
_____
_____
_____
_____
_____
_____
_____
_____
_____

I will STAY committed and FINISH the course on my journey to business ownership!

Signature: _____ Date: _____/_____/_____

THE MAXIMIZED LIFE COACHING & MENTORING WINNING TEAM MODEL
8-Week Series

JOURNAL ENTRY:

WRITE YOUR FEELINGS AS YOU CONTINUE YOUR JOURNEY TO BUSINESS OWNERSHIP

Date: ___/___/___ How do you feel about your business progress TODAY (discuss your excitement, fears, regrets, etc.)?

_____
_____
_____
_____
_____
_____
_____
_____
_____
_____
_____
_____
_____
_____
_____
_____
_____
_____
_____
_____

I will STAY committed and FINISH the course on my journey to business ownership!

Signature: _____ Date: _____/_____/_____

THE MAXIMIZED LIFE COACHING & MENTORING WINNING TEAM MODEL
8-Week Series

JOURNAL ENTRY:

WRITE YOUR FEELINGS AS YOU CONTINUE YOUR JOURNEY TO BUSINESS OWNERSHIP

Date: ___/___/___ How do you feel about your business progress TODAY (discuss your excitement, fears, regrets, etc.)?

_____
_____
_____
_____
_____
_____
_____
_____
_____
_____
_____
_____
_____
_____
_____
_____
_____
_____
_____
_____

I will STAY committed and FINISH the course on my journey to business ownership!

Signature: _____ Date: _____/_____/_____

THE MAXIMIZED LIFE COACHING & MENTORING WINNING TEAM MODEL

8-Week Series

JOURNAL ENTRY:

WRITE YOUR FEELINGS AS YOU CONTINUE YOUR JOURNEY TO BUSINESS OWNERSHIP

Date: ___/___/___ How do you feel about your business progress TODAY (discuss your excitement, fears, regrets, etc.)?

_____
_____
_____
_____
_____
_____
_____
_____
_____
_____
_____
_____
_____
_____
_____
_____
_____
_____
_____
_____

I will STAY committed and FINISH the course on my journey to business ownership!

Signature: _____ Date: _____/_____/_____

THE MAXIMIZED LIFE COACHING & MENTORING WINNING TEAM MODEL
8-Week Series

JOURNAL ENTRY:

WRITE YOUR FEELINGS AS YOU CONTINUE YOUR JOURNEY TO BUSINESS OWNERSHIP

Date: ___/___/___ How do you feel about your business progress TODAY (discuss your excitement, fears, regrets, etc.)?

_____
_____
_____
_____
_____
_____
_____
_____
_____
_____
_____
_____
_____
_____
_____
_____
_____
_____
_____
_____

I will STAY committed and FINISH the course on my journey to business ownership!

Signature: _____ Date: _____/_____/_____

THE MAXIMIZED LIFE COACHING & MENTORING WINNING TEAM MODEL
8-Week Series

JOURNAL ENTRY:

WRITE YOUR FEELINGS AS YOU CONTINUE YOUR JOURNEY TO BUSINESS OWNERSHIP

Date: ___/___/___ How do you feel about your business progress TODAY (discuss your excitement, fears, regrets, etc.)?

_____
_____
_____
_____
_____
_____
_____
_____
_____
_____
_____
_____
_____
_____
_____
_____
_____
_____
_____
_____

I will STAY committed and FINISH the course on my journey to business ownership!

Signature: _____ Date: ____/____/____

THE MAXIMIZED LIFE COACHING & MENTORING WINNING TEAM MODEL

8-Week Series

JOURNAL ENTRY:

WRITE YOUR FEELINGS AS YOU CONTINUE YOUR JOURNEY TO BUSINESS OWNERSHIP

Date: ___/___/___ How do you feel about your business progress TODAY (discuss your excitement, fears, regrets, etc.)?

_____
_____
_____
_____
_____
_____
_____
_____
_____
_____
_____
_____
_____
_____
_____
_____
_____
_____
_____
_____

I will STAY committed and FINISH the course on my journey to business ownership!

Signature: _____ Date: _____/_____/_____

THE MAXIMIZED LIFE COACHING & MENTORING WINNING TEAM MODEL

8-Week Series

JOURNAL ENTRY:

WRITE YOUR FEELINGS AS YOU CONTINUE YOUR JOURNEY TO BUSINESS OWNERSHIP

Date: ___/___/___ How do you feel about your business progress TODAY (discuss your excitement, fears, regrets, etc.)?

_____
_____
_____
_____
_____
_____
_____
_____
_____
_____
_____
_____
_____
_____
_____
_____
_____
_____
_____
_____

I will STAY committed and FINISH the course on my journey to business ownership!

Signature: _____ Date: _____/_____/_____

THE MAXIMIZED LIFE COACHING & MENTORING WINNING TEAM MODEL
8-Week Series

JOURNAL ENTRY:

WRITE YOUR FEELINGS AS YOU CONTINUE YOUR JOURNEY TO BUSINESS OWNERSHIP

Date: ___/___/___ How do you feel about your business progress TODAY (discuss your excitement, fears, regrets, etc.)?

_____
_____
_____
_____
_____
_____
_____
_____
_____
_____
_____
_____
_____
_____
_____
_____
_____
_____
_____
_____
_____
_____

I will STAY committed and FINISH the course on my journey to business ownership!

Signature: _____ Date: _____/_____/_____

THE MAXIMIZED LIFE COACHING & MENTORING WINNING TEAM MODEL
8-Week Series

JOURNAL ENTRY:

WRITE YOUR FEELINGS AS YOU CONTINUE YOUR JOURNEY TO BUSINESS OWNERSHIP

Date: ___/___/___ How do you feel about your business progress TODAY (discuss your excitement, fears, regrets, etc.)?

_____
_____
_____
_____
_____
_____
_____
_____
_____
_____
_____
_____
_____
_____
_____
_____
_____
_____
_____
_____
_____
_____

I will STAY committed and FINISH the course on my journey to business ownership!

Signature: _____ Date: ____/____/____

THE MAXIMIZED LIFE COACHING & MENTORING WINNING TEAM MODEL
8-Week Series

JOURNAL ENTRY:

WRITE YOUR FEELINGS AS YOU CONTINUE YOUR JOURNEY TO BUSINESS OWNERSHIP

Date: ___/___/___ How do you feel about your business progress TODAY (discuss your excitement, fears, regrets, etc.)?

_____
_____
_____
_____
_____
_____
_____
_____
_____
_____
_____
_____
_____
_____
_____
_____
_____
_____
_____
_____

I will STAY committed and FINISH the course on my journey to business ownership!

Signature: _____ Date: _____/_____/_____

THE MAXIMIZED LIFE COACHING & MENTORING WINNING TEAM MODEL
8-Week Series

JOURNAL ENTRY:

WRITE YOUR FEELINGS AS YOU CONTINUE YOUR JOURNEY TO BUSINESS OWNERSHIP

Date: ___/___/___ How do you feel about your business progress TODAY (discuss your excitement, fears, regrets, etc.)?

_____
_____
_____
_____
_____
_____
_____
_____
_____
_____
_____
_____
_____
_____
_____
_____
_____
_____
_____
_____

I will STAY committed and FINISH the course on my journey to business ownership!

Signature: _____ Date: _____/_____/_____

THE MAXIMIZED LIFE COACHING & MENTORING WINNING TEAM MODEL

8-Week Series

JOURNAL ENTRY:

WRITE YOUR FEELINGS AS YOU CONTINUE YOUR JOURNEY TO BUSINESS OWNERSHIP

Date: ___/___/___ How do you feel about your business progress TODAY (discuss your excitement, fears, regrets, etc.)?

_____
_____
_____
_____
_____
_____
_____
_____
_____
_____
_____
_____
_____
_____
_____
_____
_____
_____
_____
_____

I will STAY committed and FINISH the course on my journey to business ownership!

Signature: _____ Date: _____/_____/_____

THE MAXIMIZED LIFE COACHING & MENTORING WINNING TEAM MODEL
8-Week Series

JOURNAL ENTRY:

WRITE YOUR FEELINGS AS YOU CONTINUE YOUR JOURNEY TO BUSINESS OWNERSHIP

Date: ___/___/___ How do you feel about your business progress TODAY (discuss your excitement, fears, regrets, etc.)?

_____
_____
_____
_____
_____
_____
_____
_____
_____
_____
_____
_____
_____
_____
_____
_____
_____
_____
_____
_____

I will STAY committed and FINISH the course on my journey to business ownership!

Signature: _____ Date: _____/_____/_____

THE MAXIMIZED LIFE COACHING & MENTORING WINNING TEAM MODEL
8-Week Series

JOURNAL ENTRY:

WRITE YOUR FEELINGS AS YOU CONTINUE YOUR JOURNEY TO BUSINESS OWNERSHIP

Date: ___/___/___ How do you feel about your business progress TODAY (discuss your excitement, fears, regrets, etc.)?

_____
_____
_____
_____
_____
_____
_____
_____
_____
_____
_____
_____
_____
_____
_____
_____
_____
_____
_____
_____
_____
_____

I will STAY committed and FINISH the course on my journey to business ownership!

Signature: _____ Date: _____/_____/_____

THE MAXIMIZED LIFE COACHING & MENTORING WINNING TEAM MODEL
8-Week Series

JOURNAL ENTRY:

WRITE YOUR FEELINGS AS YOU CONTINUE YOUR JOURNEY TO BUSINESS OWNERSHIP

Date: ___/___/___ How do you feel about your business progress TODAY (discuss your excitement, fears, regrets, etc.)?

_____
_____
_____
_____
_____
_____
_____
_____
_____
_____
_____
_____
_____
_____
_____
_____
_____
_____
_____

I will STAY committed and FINISH the course on my journey to business ownership!

Signature: _____ Date: _____/_____/_____

THE MAXIMIZED LIFE COACHING & MENTORING WINNING TEAM MODEL
8-Week Series

JOURNAL ENTRY:

WRITE YOUR FEELINGS AS YOU CONTINUE YOUR JOURNEY TO BUSINESS OWNERSHIP

Date: ___/___/___ How do you feel about your business progress TODAY (discuss your excitement, fears, regrets, etc.)?

_____
_____
_____
_____
_____
_____
_____
_____
_____
_____
_____
_____
_____
_____
_____
_____
_____
_____
_____
_____
_____

I will STAY committed and FINISH the course on my journey to business ownership!

Signature: _____ Date: _____/_____/_____

THE MAXIMIZED LIFE COACHING & MENTORING WINNING TEAM MODEL
8-Week Series

JOURNAL ENTRY:

WRITE YOUR FEELINGS AS YOU CONTINUE YOUR JOURNEY TO BUSINESS OWNERSHIP

Date: ___/___/___ How do you feel about your business progress TODAY (discuss your excitement, fears, regrets, etc.)?

_____
_____
_____
_____
_____
_____
_____
_____
_____
_____
_____
_____
_____
_____
_____
_____
_____
_____
_____
_____
_____

I will STAY committed and FINISH the course on my journey to business ownership!

Signature: _____ Date: _____/_____/_____

THE MAXIMIZED LIFE COACHING & MENTORING WINNING TEAM MODEL

8-Week Series

JOURNAL ENTRY:

WRITE YOUR FEELINGS AS YOU CONTINUE YOUR JOURNEY TO BUSINESS OWNERSHIP

Date: ___/___/___ How do you feel about your business progress TODAY (discuss your excitement, fears, regrets, etc.)?

_____
_____
_____
_____
_____
_____
_____
_____
_____
_____
_____
_____
_____
_____
_____
_____
_____
_____
_____
_____
_____
_____

I will STAY committed and FINISH the course on my journey to business ownership!

Signature: _____ Date: _____/_____/_____

THE MAXIMIZED LIFE COACHING & MENTORING WINNING TEAM MODEL
8-Week Series

JOURNAL ENTRY:

WRITE YOUR FEELINGS AS YOU CONTINUE YOUR JOURNEY TO BUSINESS OWNERSHIP

Date: ___/___/___ How do you feel about your business progress TODAY (discuss your excitement, fears, regrets, etc.)?

_____
_____
_____
_____
_____
_____
_____
_____
_____
_____
_____
_____
_____
_____
_____
_____
_____
_____

I will STAY committed and FINISH the course on my journey to business ownership!

Signature: _____ Date: ____/____/____

THE MAXIMIZED LIFE COACHING & MENTORING WINNING TEAM MODEL
8-Week Series

JOURNAL ENTRY:

WRITE YOUR FEELINGS AS YOU CONTINUE YOUR JOURNEY TO BUSINESS OWNERSHIP

Date: ___/___/___ How do you feel about your business progress TODAY (discuss your excitement, fears, regrets, etc.)?

_____
_____
_____
_____
_____
_____
_____
_____
_____
_____
_____
_____
_____
_____
_____
_____
_____
_____
_____
_____

I will STAY committed and FINISH the course on my journey to business ownership!

Signature: _____ Date: _____/_____/_____

THE MAXIMIZED LIFE COACHING & MENTORING WINNING TEAM MODEL
8-Week Series

JOURNAL ENTRY:

WRITE YOUR FEELINGS AS YOU CONTINUE YOUR JOURNEY TO BUSINESS OWNERSHIP

Date: ___/___/___ How do you feel about your business progress TODAY (discuss your excitement, fears, regrets, etc.)?

_____
_____
_____
_____
_____
_____
_____
_____
_____
_____
_____
_____
_____
_____
_____
_____
_____
_____
_____
_____

I will STAY committed and FINISH the course on my journey to business ownership!

Signature: _____ Date: _____/_____/_____

THE MAXIMIZED LIFE COACHING & MENTORING WINNING TEAM MODEL
8-Week Series

JOURNAL ENTRY:

WRITE YOUR FEELINGS AS YOU CONTINUE YOUR JOURNEY TO BUSINESS OWNERSHIP

Date: ___/___/___ How do you feel about your business progress TODAY (discuss your excitement, fears, regrets, etc.)?

_____
_____
_____
_____
_____
_____
_____
_____
_____
_____
_____
_____
_____
_____
_____
_____
_____
_____
_____
_____

I will STAY committed and FINISH the course on my journey to business ownership!

Signature: _____ Date: _____/_____/_____

THE MAXIMIZED LIFE COACHING & MENTORING WINNING TEAM MODEL
8-Week Series

JOURNAL ENTRY:

WRITE YOUR FEELINGS AS YOU CONTINUE YOUR JOURNEY TO BUSINESS OWNERSHIP

Date: ___/___/___ How do you feel about your business progress TODAY (discuss your excitement, fears, regrets, etc.)?

_____
_____
_____
_____
_____
_____
_____
_____
_____
_____
_____
_____
_____
_____
_____
_____
_____
_____

I will STAY committed and FINISH the course on my journey to business ownership!

Signature: _____ Date: ____/____/____

THE MAXIMIZED LIFE COACHING & MENTORING WINNING TEAM MODEL
8-Week Series

JOURNAL ENTRY:

WRITE YOUR FEELINGS AS YOU CONTINUE YOUR JOURNEY TO BUSINESS OWNERSHIP

Date: ___/___/___ How do you feel about your business progress TODAY (discuss your excitement, fears, regrets, etc.)?

_____
_____
_____
_____
_____
_____
_____
_____
_____
_____
_____
_____
_____
_____
_____
_____
_____
_____
_____
_____

I will STAY committed and FINISH the course on my journey to business ownership!

Signature: _____ Date: _____/_____/_____

THE MAXIMIZED LIFE COACHING & MENTORING WINNING TEAM MODEL

8-Week Series

JOURNAL ENTRY:

WRITE YOUR FEELINGS AS YOU CONTINUE YOUR JOURNEY TO BUSINESS OWNERSHIP

Date: ___/___/___ How do you feel about your business progress TODAY (discuss your excitement, fears, regrets, etc.)?

_____
_____
_____
_____
_____
_____
_____
_____
_____
_____
_____
_____
_____
_____
_____
_____
_____
_____
_____
_____
_____
_____
_____
_____

I will STAY committed and FINISH the course on my journey to business ownership!

Signature: _____ Date: _____/_____/_____

THE MAXIMIZED LIFE COACHING & MENTORING WINNING TEAM MODEL
8-Week Series

JOURNAL ENTRY:

WRITE YOUR FEELINGS AS YOU CONTINUE YOUR JOURNEY TO BUSINESS OWNERSHIP

Date: ___/___/___ How do you feel about your business progress TODAY (discuss your excitement, fears, regrets, etc.)?

_____
_____
_____
_____
_____
_____
_____
_____
_____
_____
_____
_____
_____
_____
_____
_____
_____
_____
_____
_____

I will STAY committed and FINISH the course on my journey to business ownership!

Signature: _____ Date: ____/____/____

THE MAXIMIZED LIFE COACHING & MENTORING WINNING TEAM MODEL
8-Week Series

JOURNAL ENTRY:

WRITE YOUR FEELINGS AS YOU CONTINUE YOUR JOURNEY TO BUSINESS OWNERSHIP

Date: ___/___/___ How do you feel about your business progress TODAY (discuss your excitement, fears, regrets, etc.)?

_____
_____
_____
_____
_____
_____
_____
_____
_____
_____
_____
_____
_____
_____
_____
_____
_____
_____

I will STAY committed and FINISH the course on my journey to business ownership!

Signature: _____ Date: _____/_____/_____

THE MAXIMIZED LIFE COACHING & MENTORING WINNING TEAM MODEL
8-Week Series

JOURNAL ENTRY:

WRITE YOUR FEELINGS AS YOU CONTINUE YOUR JOURNEY TO BUSINESS OWNERSHIP

Date: ___/___/___ How do you feel about your business progress TODAY (discuss your excitement, fears, regrets, etc.)?

_____
_____
_____
_____
_____
_____
_____
_____
_____
_____
_____
_____
_____
_____
_____
_____
_____
_____
_____
_____
_____
_____

I will STAY committed and FINISH the course on my journey to business ownership!

Signature: _____ Date: _____/_____/_____

THE MAXIMIZED LIFE COACHING & MENTORING WINNING TEAM MODEL
8-Week Series

JOURNAL ENTRY:

WRITE YOUR FEELINGS AS YOU CONTINUE YOUR JOURNEY TO BUSINESS OWNERSHIP

Date: ___/___/___ How do you feel about your business progress TODAY (discuss your excitement, fears, regrets, etc.)?

_____
_____
_____
_____
_____
_____
_____
_____
_____
_____
_____
_____
_____
_____
_____
_____
_____
_____
_____
_____

I will STAY committed and FINISH the course on my journey to business ownership!

Signature: _____ Date: _____/_____/_____

THE MAXIMIZED LIFE COACHING & MENTORING WINNING TEAM MODEL
8-Week Series

JOURNAL ENTRY:

WRITE YOUR FEELINGS AS YOU CONTINUE YOUR JOURNEY TO BUSINESS OWNERSHIP

Date: ___/___/___ How do you feel about your business progress TODAY (discuss your excitement, fears, regrets, etc.)?

_____
_____
_____
_____
_____
_____
_____
_____
_____
_____
_____
_____
_____
_____
_____
_____
_____
_____
_____
_____

I will STAY committed and FINISH the course on my journey to business ownership!

Signature: _____ Date: ____/____/____

THE MAXIMIZED LIFE COACHING & MENTORING WINNING TEAM MODEL

8-Week Series

JOURNAL ENTRY:

WRITE YOUR FEELINGS AS YOU CONTINUE YOUR JOURNEY TO BUSINESS OWNERSHIP

Date: ___/___/___ How do you feel about your business progress TODAY (discuss your excitement, fears, regrets, etc.)?

_____
_____
_____
_____
_____
_____
_____
_____
_____
_____
_____
_____
_____
_____
_____
_____
_____
_____
_____
_____

I will STAY committed and FINISH the course on my journey to business ownership!

Signature: _____ Date: _____/_____/_____

THE MAXIMIZED LIFE COACHING & MENTORING WINNING TEAM MODEL
8-Week Series

JOURNAL ENTRY:

WRITE YOUR FEELINGS AS YOU CONTINUE YOUR JOURNEY TO BUSINESS OWNERSHIP

Date: ___/___/___ How do you feel about your business progress TODAY (discuss your excitement, fears, regrets, etc.)?

_____
_____
_____
_____
_____
_____
_____
_____
_____
_____
_____
_____
_____
_____
_____
_____
_____
_____
_____
_____

I will STAY committed and FINISH the course on my journey to business ownership!

Signature: _____ Date: _____/_____/_____

THE MAXIMIZED LIFE COACHING & MENTORING WINNING TEAM MODEL
8-Week Series

JOURNAL ENTRY:

WRITE YOUR FEELINGS AS YOU CONTINUE YOUR JOURNEY TO BUSINESS OWNERSHIP

Date: ___/___/___ How do you feel about your business progress TODAY (discuss your excitement, fears, regrets, etc.)?

_____
_____
_____
_____
_____
_____
_____
_____
_____
_____
_____
_____
_____
_____
_____
_____
_____
_____
_____
_____

I will STAY committed and FINISH the course on my journey to business ownership!

Signature: _____ Date: ____/____/____

THE MAXIMIZED LIFE COACHING & MENTORING WINNING TEAM MODEL
8-Week Series

JOURNAL ENTRY:

WRITE YOUR FEELINGS AS YOU CONTINUE YOUR JOURNEY TO BUSINESS OWNERSHIP

Date: ___/___/___ How do you feel about your business progress TODAY (discuss your excitement, fears, regrets, etc.)?

_____
_____
_____
_____
_____
_____
_____
_____
_____
_____
_____
_____
_____
_____
_____
_____
_____
_____
_____
_____
_____

I will STAY committed and FINISH the course on my journey to business ownership!

Signature: _____ Date: _____/_____/_____

THE MAXIMIZED LIFE COACHING & MENTORING WINNING TEAM MODEL

8-Week Series

The Maximized Life Coaching and Mentoring Team (the MAX Team) is a Demonstrational Life & Business Coach Program specializing in program development, strategic planning, and business structuring. The MAX Team provides Coaching and Mentoring to small business owners and contract professionals who want to take their business to another level.

The MAX Team program offers one on one support, group support, networking opportunities and business connections. The 8-Week Winning Team Model is a program offered to the business owners that the MAX Team serve.

Not only does the MAX Team coach small businesses to sUccess, we also offer space for dreams to become reality. Located in the heart of Williamsburg, Virginia, dreams are born in the MAX Building, a creative co-workspace for small businesses, young or old, to co-work and live out their visions and dreams. Small businesses have a built-in network of other small businesses that serves as a support system. MAX Coaches are available on site to help ease some of the anxieties of being a business owner and having to do business alone.

Office space as well as virtual office membership is available for those who wish to take their business to another level!

Visit our website to connect with any member of the MAX Team as well as schedule an initial FREE telephone consultation. Start your dream of business ownership TODAY!

THE MAXIMIZED LIFE COACHING & MENTORING WINNING TEAM MODEL
8-Week Series

BE A MAX TEAM MEMBER TODAY!!!

5252 OLDE TOWNE ROAD

WILLIAMSBURG, VA 23188

https://www.maximizedlifecoaching.com